Habitat

Habitat

Judith Thompson

Playwrights Canada Press
Toronto • Canada

Habitat © Copyright 2001 Judith Thompson

PLAYWRIGHTS CANADA PRESS
The Canadian Drama Publisher
215 Spadina Ave., Suite 230, Toronto, Ontario M5T 2C7
phone 416.703.0013   fax 416.408.3402
orders@playwrightscanada.com • www.playwrightscanada.com

For amateur or professional production rights, please contact
Great North Artists Management, 350 Dupont Street, Toronto, Ontario M5R 1V9
416.925.2051 • info@gnaminc.com

The publisher acknowledges the support of the Canadian taxpayers through the Government of Canada Book Publishing Industry Development Program, the Canada Council for the Arts, the Ontario Arts Council, and the Ontario Media Development Corporation.

Cover photo *Forbidden Territory* © 1996 Freeman Patterson
Production Editor/Cover Design: Jodi Armstrong

NATIONAL LIBRARY OF CANADA CATALOGUING IN PUBLICATION DATA
Thompson, Judith, 1954-
Habitat

A play.
ISBN 978-0-88754-615-0

I. Title.

PS8589.H4883H32 2002   C812'.54   C2001-902336-7
PR9199.3.T469H32 2002

First edition: October 2002
Third printing: September 2009
Printed and bound in Canada by Hignell Printing, Winnipeg

this play is dedicated to
every group home struggling to survive
in a hostile neighbourhood

PLAYWRIGHT'S NOTES

I want to thank Iris Turcott for her brilliant, fiery dramaturgy, and Katherine Kaszas and Marty Bragg and everyone at Can Stage. I want to thank especially the magnificent actors who brought this play to life: the incomparable and inspirational Stephen Ouimette; the sublime artist and cherished friend Nancy Palk; the brilliant young lion Holly Lewis; the hilarious and talented Luke Kirby; Kristina Nichol for her passion and dedication; Corinne, a more perfect Margaret I could never imagine; John Munro, for the lighting design; and Braham Murray and Sarah Frankom at the Royal Exchange for their support and strong dramaturgy and my longtime friend and truly inspirational dramaturge, Len Berkman. I would also like to thank Jodi at Playwrights Canada Press, and the magnificent Angela Rebeiro for her endless strength and wisdom, and finally my husband, Gregor, and my children Ariane, Eli, Grace, Felicity and Sophia for all the love and the patience.

INTRODUCTION

Judith Thompson's body of work is vast and varied but always visceral. In fact, it often takes your breath away or, at the very least, alters your pattern of breathing. *Crackwalker*, her first play—produced in 1980—left audiences gasping at her brutal depiction of the lives of the marginalized. Now considered one of the most important Canadian classics, it is still constantly produced, still utterly relevant, and still breathtaking.

Indeed, whenever I think about Judith and her work, I think of breath. I remember when Judith read, for the first time, what would become the opening scene of *Habitat*. A woman lying in a hospital bed is struggling to breathe while her daughter struggles to communicate her fear, pain and guilt in a barrage of mundane, adolescent outbursts. The halting and unexpected rhythms, so rife with subtext, build to a fever pitch and the scene moves onto a heightened theatrical landscape that lies somewhere between the conscious and the unconscious, a place that is neither past nor present and where mother and daughter achieve a poetic, symbiotic state of shared breath – of shared life. It is a moment of sheer beauty but, in typical Thompson form, the moment is shattered by a brutal shift back to "reality."

It was an astounding first draft of a first scene which Judith read perfectly. It is not just that she is an accomplished actress but also that she inhabits her characters so her knowledge of them is profound. In fact, she has said as much, "I am written in my plays whether I want to be or not. My breath is their breath." First drafts for Judith are an act of faith and she goes blindly wherever her instincts lead her. This critical first scene in *Habitat* led her to complete a first draft in which the word breath or breathing occurred countless times whether in the text proper or the stage directions. Each character also had their own idiosyncratic obsessions with breathing which collectively articulated her thematic exploration of physical, psychic, and spiritual survival and how they are linked.

In *Habitat* Judith holds the mirror up to our world where property values collide with human values. It forces us to examine what we consider our personal standard for "survival" and who and what we are prepared to sacrifice to pay the price. Who will suffocate because we need to breathe? *Habitat* is a brutal examination of the society in which we live but ultimately it is a cry for personal and social change.

—Iris Turcott, Dramaturge
Canadian Stage Company, Toronto, Canada

Habitat was co-commissioned by Canadian Stage Company, Toronto and The Royal Exchange Theatre in Manchester, England. It premiered at the Bluma Appel Theatre on Sept. 20, 2001 with the following company:

LEWIS CHANCE	Stephen Ouimette
RAINE	Holly Lewis
SPARKLE	Luke Kirby
MARGARET	Corinne Conley
JANET	Kristina Nicholl

Directed by Katherine Kaszas
Set and Costumes designed by Shawn Kerwin
Lighting designed by John Munro
Sound designed by Richard Feren
Stage Managed by Linda Matassa
Assistant Director: Rebecca Brown
Assistant Stage Manager: Tobi Hunt
Assistant to the Playwright: Caroline Azar

Habitat was workshopped in December 2000 with the above cast, (except Kristina Nicholl; Nancy Palk originated the role of Janet) directed by Judith Thompson. It was produced in Manchester, England in November 2002.

CHARACTERS

LEWIS CHANCE
RAINE
SPARKLE
MARGARET
JANET

ACT ONE

—— 1 ——

A woman in her forties, CATH, is dying of cancer.
We hear her struggling to breathe throughout
the scene. Her 16-year-old daughter, RAINE, is
hovering in the doorway.

RAINE   I can't stay too long today, I'm supposed to be
meeting Crystal and Ginnie at the Eaton Centre.

CATH is too weak to answer. A few moments.
RAINE just wants to run out but she forces
herself to stay. She looks at her mother's now
grotesque face.

Dad and Patrice are coming later. At least, that's
what they said.

Beat.

I told Dad I'm not living with him and Patrice;
there is no way I am going to live in Cornwall,
I would rather kill myself.

I'm living with Crystal in Cabbagetown. Her
mum said it was fine. They are like totally cool
with it. I mean CORNWALL. God.

So Mum? You have to tell Dad it's okay for me to
live with Crystal, okay?

Could you tell him that when he comes in later?
TONIGHT. Cause like, he won't listen to me, he
just yells and screams and turns really red and
I really don't want to live in Cornwall. Your lips
are like so cracked.

CATH struggles to breathe.

All of my friends are here.

Oh. By the way. I'm getting these new jeans today. They're really nice. Way better than the ones I have; the ones I have are like three years old. These ones? Look very good on me. So... Mum, Can I – use your credit card? To get them? Or just take your bank card and get some money and then bring it back? You know, money is a real problem for me these days. They won't even give me money for lunch Patrice packs like this baloney sandwich for me and expects me to actually eat it; of course, it goes right into the garbage.

You should really tell the nurse to brush your hair. It like so needs it. It's funny me tellin' you to brush your hair, eh? Used to be you yelling at me "Rainey you cannot go out of this house with hair like a homeless person!" and then you would like attack me with brush.

CATH's breathing is very bad.

I am going to tell Dad he has to brush your hair. He can look at all this dandruff. He can change your diaper thing too, he should do some of those things when he is here. Huh. He's probably too busy feeling up Patrice while the two of them are here. He can't keep his hands off her it is so gross; I can even HEAR them sometimes when I stay there? You have never heard anything so gross in your life as the sound of her... God. I would rather walk into a toilet stall and see somebody's tampon on top of their shit, you know?

Patrice tried to have some big talk with me. She's like: "you understand your mother is very very sick" I'm like "Oh really Patrice?" and she's like "Honey," (she calls me "honey") "are you pre-pared?" And I'm like, "PREPARED?" "Oh my God, bitch, your hairdo is so eighties I think I am going to throw up in your face!"

So, I'm going to take your bank card then. And
I'll take a little bit more than what the jeans cost.
Because you do owe me for six allowances.

> CATH *has trouble breathing.*

(very quietly) Look. I know you are sick, Mom. But
you know what? I know you are not quite as sick
as you're pretending to be. *(beat)* You've ALWAYS
exaggerated how sick you are you have always
done that, just to like make me stick around and
feel sorry for you and like, not go to my raves or
whatever. Well I'll tell you something. I feel sorry
for you but I don't feel that sorry for you.

> CATH'S *breathing is more laboured.*

Oh my God it's quarter to seven. I really gotta go.
I just hope Crystal and Ginnie don't start getting
all weird on me. "Is your mum okay? Oh that's so
sad." People are so – like if anybody mentions
like mothers, or cancer, everybody is like "shhhh
oh my God, look what's happening to Raine, her
mother is dying." And their faces they have this
expression I feel like just slapping it off them,
you know? I'm like what am I supposed to be
feeling here? Is there something I'm supposed
to be feeling?

> CATH *struggles for breath. A few long moments.*
> RAINE *gets the credit card.*

I mean I know you're my mother, and you'd
think I should be all choked up and maybe
I should be but the truth is that you, all I know
of you, like before this, is that sharp face of yours
and your sharp, nasty voice bitching out at me for
everything, for being late, or going to the movies,
or getting my belly pierced, not cleaning my
room, or not coming home enough and you
always do it in the voice, the knife-voice right,
like you are knifing me with your voice, right?
And I have come to hate your voice you know?
you know? And I kinda like things this way,

because you're so quiet for once in your life. I get to do the talking and I really really like that. And you get to listen.

I don't even have anything to wear to your funeral. I have like one pair of shoes. Like, what am I supposed to wear? One of your dresses, those skanky smelling old hippie dresses of yours from like thirty years ago? No thank you. No. No. I just have nothing. Not one black dress. I don't know, do you want me to wear black? Do people still do that? Oh God. They'll all be staring at me. Looking for the tears.

Sounds of distress from Cath.

You're not the only person in the world who's been through this. You are not the only tragic figure in the world. I was right where you are, remember? Or maybe you don't remember that.

Suddenly, Cath jolts upright and grabs RAINE's hands.

CATH   Oh my God. Oh my God.

RAINE   That Sunday night when I was a baby Sunday when you tried to breast feed I fell off your breast!

CATH   Oh my God, Gerald? She fell off my breast; she's too weak to nurse, she fell off the breast she's NEVER done THAT come on, baby, nurse, please baby come on.

RAINE   Disappearing! I could feel myself disappearing–

Cath takes RAINE in her arms.

CATH   Shall we take her to the hospital? They'll make us wait all night, I thought it was just a virus, they said she would be be fine, she's not fine, she looks like a dying baby – should we wait until morning? She might be DEAD by morning–

RAINE   –and I lay beside you my face in your neck breathing with you and I dreamed I was drowning–

CATH   –and I couldn't breathe in my dream and I was way underwater and and and oh my GOD she isn't breathing–

RAINE   –no breathing disappearing disappearing–

CATH   –I was you, I was dreaming I was you, not breathing then breathing; in my dreaming: breathing lighter and lighter; so still so still almost gone and–

RAINE   –barely breathing–

CATH   –911.

RAINE   –rushed into a bed with monitors: heart, oxygen saturation, an oxygen mask. I remember mother I remember and oh my God… low oxygen, dehydrated this is very serious she is sick didn't you know how sick she was? Didn't you know this baby is sick?

CATH   Let me have her, please, I want to nurse her–

RAINE   You might lose her–

CATH   –might lose her? No no no no no no no.

RAINE   I might choke, Cathy, choke on your MILK–

CATH   I have lost my milk! I have LOST MY MILK!!

RAINE   –and the nurses with gowns and with masks they rolled me onto my throne in the ICU all the needles inside me for breathing *(breathing sound)* and feeding and a heart and a breathing and and waters and a nurse and you with your scared eyes, pacing, unbrushed hair, pacing, talking to me saying my name over and over "Rainey Rainey, mummy's here!"

CATH	Mummy's here, Rainey, Mummy's here. "Gentle Rainey, gentle girl, sweet and loving little pearl–"
RAINE	I can't make a sound, the breathing tube, shoved down my throat I'm riding the respirator–
CATH	–the machine is breathing for her she's not breathing at all.
RAINE	–and I cry and I cry with no voice no voice–
CATH	Is she crying? Is she trying to cry and making no sound? Because of the tube? Oh my God oh my God. She can't even hear herself cry!
RAINE	–and the voices and shadows and the sound of the breathing and the off-key songs you sang and the washing of hands and you. When you were finally composing the death notice what you would say to your friends I breathed again, *(beat)* on my own with no help from you.

> *RAINE moves out of the trance and away from CATH. Cath comes to consciousness, and groggily looks at RAINE.*

CATH	Hello Rainey.

> *Pause – RAINE is shocked to hear her mother speak.*

What time is it?

RAINE	I really gotta go. Are you...?
CATH	Tired. *(She reaches for RAINE.)* You look pretty. How'd I get... such... a pretty... girl?

> *RAINE stares awhile, but cannot bring herself to hug her.*

RAINE	Crystal and Ginny are waiting for me at the McDonalds. Crystal gets so mad when she is kept waiting. And she is my partner for this civics

project we are working on, it's worth 50% of the
final mark. So like I don't want her to be... you
know, pissed at me anyways I really gotta go
so – see you when I see you.

—— 2 ——

We are with LEWIS Chance. He speaks to the
audience with a live microphone as if they are the
gathered residents of Mapleview Lanes. He is in a
high school auditorium.

LEWIS   Ladies and gentlemen; neighbours and friends.
Good evening! Hey, I want to thank you for com-
ing out on this raw and windy night isn't that terrible? Took my new hat right offa my head! Oh
hey I hope you have helped yourselves to the
delicious pineapple upside-down squares made
by Darlene, one of your future neighbours, and
the coffee made by, well, me, or really the late
great Timothy Horton! What a hockey player, eh?
That's how old I am, I remember! So these
refreshments are for... your refreshment. Yah! SO.
Here I am, your new noisy neighbour, the guy
everyone has been talking about, Lewis Chance.
I haven't been on a high school stage since I was
in *Guys and Dolls* at Lord Beaverbrook High 1971
(*sings*) "I got the horse right here, his name is
Paul Revere and here's a guy who says if the
weather's clear... can do...." Now I invited you
all here so that we could, you know, get to know
each other, chew the fat, tell a few bad jokes
because hey, we're gonna be neighbours for the
next fifty years. That's right I'm not going anywhere for a long long time because I, Lewis
Chance, have purchased a home on your exclusive Mapleview Lanes. You'd better believe it.
I paid 640,000 dollars for it and I paid it in cash.
Yes. I, Lewis Chance, who grew up in rural New
Brunswick, and have lived in rat-infested
Parkdale rooming houses and illegal basement
apartments all over the city, have bought a house
in one of the finest neighbourhoods in Etobicoke,

a neighbourhood of accomplished and distinguished and really well-dressed, well shod people. For me this is a miracle. So. I won't dilly-
dally I will get right to the point; there have been
a heck of a lot of rumours sweeping around in the
last few months. I am here to tell you that the
house will be my home!

Yes. With the hugely enthusiastic support of the
Children's Aid and the Ministry who is wisely
privatizing a whack of Social Services—thank
God, because they were in a colossal mess, as you
know—I, an old-style social worker who's been
bustin' my butt on the front lines for twenty-five
years, running homes like this one for the last ten,
I am opening my arms and my new home to a
few of the the teenagers of this city Yup…. There
will be 12 teenagers between the ages of 12 and
18 living among you on your Mapleview Lanes.
And let me tell ya…. This will be a real home. I
will be there full time assisted by the best super-
visors in the city Marge and Ted Tracy, there will
be no trouble in this group home. And I know,
listen, I know this is an exclusive street, guys, I
am not naive. I mean Hey, I know that the reason
most of you are here, sittin' in front of me is
because you want to stop this. It makes ya
uneasy. Of course. Stands to reason. You want to
stop Lewis Chance from running a group home
on your fantastically beautiful tree-lined Mapleview Lanes. Who could blame you? A lot of
group homes are terrible! We've all heard the
stories of kids goin' out of control those are the
stories the newspapers LOVE, right? And so a lot
of you guys, you're talking petitions, and city hall
and lawyers, you fear the teens because you do
not know them, you fear for your house prices,
thinkin' they'll go down, way down, and
Mapleview Lanes in ten twenty years will be a
city SLUM and you won't be able to afford your
retirement condominium by the water this is
understandable! You fear the weeds might grow
on the lawn you fear the paint might peel on the
house and most of all you fear, we all fear the

eyes of these lost boys and girls. You know that
they are troubled girls and boys, otherwise they
wouldn't be comin into a group home, now
would they? You know that they are VERY angry,
full of adolescent rage at their situation, and you
know that they are mostly unrefined girls and
boys, from un-refined homes. Not like your own
teenagers, who have the good manners and the
good haircuts and the good shoes these girls and
boys do not have good anything. They are the
lost ones, the ones that nobody cared about. The
ones who were beaten, or raped every night, or
used to make pornographic films just a few miles
from your fine homes, think about it, or at best?
Neglected, abandoned, left when they were two
years old in the care of a ten-year-old brother for
weeks and weeks, these are the ones who are
called "bastard" and "whore" by their cracked
out mother every day of their lives, screamed at
for breathing, or using the bathroom, screamed at
for breathing; these are the ones who come to
their schools with greasy and unbrushed hair and
dark circles under their eyes and yellowing skin;
these are the ones with the bony bodies who fall
sound asleep in class teacher can't wake them up
no boots in the winter no winter coats the children who never speak up they are not in the
French Club or the Ski Club or the Band. These
are the children who are all alone.

And Lewis Chance wants to bring them home.

I want to bring these children we have failed—oh
yes, every one of us has failed them, me and you
and you and you—onto your Mapleview Lanes
and into your lives. I want to bring them into a
house like the houses my mother cleaned every
day of her life, roomy, airy and full of light. I'm
going to bring them into this house and I'm going
to say "This is your home." "This is your home
boys and girls. Now and forever. This is your
home." And I guess what I'm here to ask you
guys is – you know? I feel like I'm one of those
early explorers heading into this, big new world,

and and what I want to ask you is something we
say down in the Maritimes, I want to ask you,
"Are you comin' with? Are you – comin' with?"

———— 3 ————

*The living room of MARGARET Deacon's home.
Once a splendid and perfect living room it is now
in a horrendous state, due to her depression aris-
ing from her husband's death two years ago. There
is a knocking on the door. MARGARET, a wreck
in a housecoat, is writing thank you cards.*

JANET   *(off-stage)* Mum? Hellooo? Mum? Mum it's Janet.
Mum! Hello. Mum Please, it's me, I only have a
few minutes, MUM? Mum I really don't want to
break in but if you don't answer, – MUM? Oh my
God. MUUUUUUUUUUM? O.K. O.K.

*Sound of window breaking or opening. JANET
climbs in a window, and falls to the ground.*

Mum! You're here. Why… why didn't you open
the door for me, Mum, I was out there knocking
for a half an hour.

MARGARET is silent, angry.

It's freezing out there, Mummy, and I was wor-
ried about you; last time you didn't answer the
door or the phone you had had a heart attack –
are you… you are alright, aren't you? Mum?
Mum?

MARGARET   DON'T touch me.

JANET   Oh Mummy. Mummy, are you–

MARGARET   You – broke – into my house.

JANET   But you wouldn't answer the door, what was
I supposed to do, call the police? I didn't want to
call the police and and frighten you, I thought
I would just–

MARGARET   YOU BROKE INTO MY HOUSE. Steven and
           Marjorie would NEVER–

JANET   Steven and Marjorie live a thousand miles away,
           Mum, it's me who is here for you, who comes to
           make sure you are…

           I mean why. Did you not. Answer the door.

MARGARET   Because. I am… busy. VERY busy. I have one
           hundred and thirteen thank you cards left to
           write, I have only written and sent 60; it's been
           more than two years and I…

JANET   Oh Mummy, Mummy! People do understand,
           you know, after what you've been through?
           NOBODY expects you to – oh my God my panty
           hose look at that RUN. *(She takes off her panty hose,
           grabs another pair from her purse and puts it on.)*

MARGARET   The people I know very much EXPECT a thank
           you card my dear. What ARE you doing, Janet?

JANET   Putting on a fresh pair of panty hose, Mum.

MARGARET   To not write your thank you cards is social
           suicide or is that idea part of your feminism?

JANET   Well – hmm. I don't know, Mum, I mean yes, it is
           nice to say "thank you," but really, why does it
           always fall on the–

MARGARET   It's gone too far if you ask me. These young fire-
           brands who – who refuse to take their husband's
           name? Oh it just infuriates me. If they had any
           idea what your father's generation sacrificed,
           how many kind and gentle men DIED in the air,
           on the sea, in the trenches so that these little
           TWITS could speak their minds… and and SPIT
           on their father's graves, I…

JANET   Oooh. Somebody I know is – a prickly today! Did
           you eat yet?

MARGARET   None of your business. You should be worrying about your children's nourishment, not mine.

JANET   Mummy, Bethany and Hamish eat at school, you know that.

MARGARET   I'm not hungry for food anymore can't even look at it.

JANET   But you are looking so frail, really – you are a wraith, Mummy I know! I KNOW. What if I pay Rowena to make meals for you and freeze them; that way you could–

MARGARET   I don't like her cooking its too spicy.

JANET   Oh Mum.

MARGARET   And you know I don't like your cooking.

JANET   God no. Even I don't like my cooking.

MARGARET   I simply could not cope with cleaning a pot, Janet, are you going to force me to...

JANET   No! God, of course not, sweetie, you need, you DESERVE a cleaning lady, Mum. Listen, Peggy Creese does wonderful work for me – she gets down on her hands and knees–

MARGARET   –Absolutely not.

JANET   –and and scrubs till you can see your face in the FLOOR, I mean...

MARGARET   How dare you comment on the state of my house anyway.

JANET   MUM. Really. Just... I mean... look around you. Please. These floors – you have not swept the floors since he died. Have you? I mean... what is this white dust? That is you, your skin, all over the floor, as if you were, I don't know, ROTTING in here, and and one day, I'll come in and you will just be dust.... This is all like some kind of nightmare. Of disintegration. The car, just sitting there, dead, in the driveway. The dirty counters, the floors, covered in your white dust. These newspapers piled to the ceiling these bills all these bills you haven't looked at in months bills which could render you homeless. You – Once the most chic and elegant, now, oh Mum He has been dead for two years don't you think it's time you–

MARGARET –Get out.

JANET Mother, I am here, and I am going to help you whether you like it or not. *(She is picking up stuff, clearing.)* You can scream at me and you can call me horrible names but I am going to do what simply has to be done. I cannot stand by any longer and let you live in this unhealthy, unsanitary – dangerous–

MARGARET *(overlapping)* LOOK to your own MESS and LEAVE MINE ALONE you clean up your own house for heaven's sake go and give your poor lonely children some of your time you selfish twit no, you stay... away... from...

    JANET is looking through bills MARGARET considers private.

No! you are not to touch any of my papers! Janet Catherine you put that back this INSTANT you...

Get out. This is my house. LEAVE. LEAVE MY HOUSE NOW. Can't you understand I want to be left alone! I want to be left alone! Alone! Just LEAVE ME ALONE!!

JANET You crazy, demented Bitch! I won't be back for a long time! You understand? You are on your OWN, Mummy, you are ON your OWN!!

    JANET leaves. She calls her husband on her cell phone.

Hi, it's me. Terrible. I totally screwed it up, I'm a
complete stupid idiot, she thought I was criticiz-
ing. She kept jabbing at me, the way she does,
and then I tried to clean for her, I mean Michael,
the place is beyond the beyond and she lost it,
started attacking me, yeah, hitting me! and I...
I don't know, I flipped. No of course I didn't hit
her, she hit me, but I yelled. I called her a bitch –
I don't know, when I'm with her I just can't seem
to control myself why? Why is it I become a
twelve-year-old girl around her? Oh Michael
don't forget about Bethany's violin lesson. Five
o'clock, and Hamish has soccer at 6:30, yeah,
I told you I'll be at a meeting till 8:00. Yeah. Uh
huh. Love you.

> RAINE appears in MARGARET's house. RAINE
> is turning in circles, with her arms out, as if she is
> imitating a helicopter while JANET speaks on the
> cell phone. During JANET's conversation, she
> falls to the ground, and wakes up as soon as
> JANET is finished.

—— 4 ——

RAINE   Is this number 237 Mapleview Lanes?

Is this number 237...? Is this number...?

MARGARET Who are you? What do you want?

RAINE   Is this..?

MARGARET Take whatever you want but don't touch – my
wedding pictures – they aren't of any use to
you... I think there is about 3000 dollars on my
dresser with the cosmetics–

RAINE   What? (*RAINE feels like she's going to throw up.*)

MARGARET You look awfully young to be committing a
robbery, has someone put you up to it? Someone
from the apartments?

RAINE   Who – who – are you, are you um. You think I'm
               a… or are you… *(consults paper)* Marge? You
               aren't Marge are you?

MARGARET   You poor child. You're only a very young girl.
               Your father, or an older brother from the apart-
               ments has put you up to this, hasn't he?

RAINE   Is this… 237?

MARGARET   237?

RAINE   237 Mapleview Lanes?

MARGARET   No. No, dear this is 207. Did you mean to rob
               237?

RAINE   You know, you really shouldn't be scared of me,
               I love old ladies, I loved my gramma she used to
               wear white gloves – and drink Lapsang Souchong
               tea.

MARGARET   –How old did you say you were?

RAINE   16.

MARGARET   And what… who… are you looking for?

RAINE   The group home? At 237?

MARGARET   Group home? You are looking for a group home?
               Here? On Mapleview Lanes?

RAINE   Yeah. At 237.

MARGARET   Oh no, dear, I think you must be mistaken. Now
               there might be a group home past the apartments,
               over the marsh–

RAINE   No. It's 237 Mapleview Lanes. Look.

               She shows her an official booklet/document,
               with her name in large letters on the front.

> *MARGARET reads in horror. She is so horrified she cannot speak.*

Do you know it?

MARGARET Number 237. Yes. Oh yes I know it well.

RAINE Yeah. Is it nice?

MARGARET I can't believe it.

RAINE What?

> *MARGARET gets her breath and composure.*

MARGARET The Alexanders'. Is now a group home. *(She looks at RAINE's bag.)* And you are going to live there. Dear child. Tell me. Why would you be going to live in a "group home." I can hear breeding under that slovenly speech, and I see years of ballet lessons in your carriage; do you mind if I ask you what happened?

RAINE ...my Mother. She died.

MARGARET You poor child. How old was your mother when she—

RAINE —42, I think.

MARGARET Oh God in heaven.

RAINE What?

MARGARET Well I've just lost my husband, two years ago; every day I wake up feeling as though I have been battered.

RAINE Is that why the house is... you know...

MARGARET I suppose. It's in a dreadful state, isn't it?

RAINE   I don't mind it. It's like my room. Was. My
               mother, she woulda hated it.

MARGARET   When did your mother die?

RAINE   On May 17th. It was hot.

MARGARET   My husband died in the winter.

RAINE   I wasn't there. When she died.

MARGARET   Neither was I. He waited until I had gone home.

RAINE   I was at the Eaton Centre. Buying these jeans.

MARGARET   I'm sure you loved your mother very much.

RAINE   Not really.

MARGARET   I'm sure she died knowing how much you loved
               her.

RAINE   Nope.

MARGARET   Why do you say that?

RAINE   Because I didn't. Love her.

MARGARET   Of course you did. She was your mother. You
               were her daughter. Believe me. You loved your
               mother.

RAINE   I think I better go. *(She walks to the door.)*

MARGARET   Where... where is your father, dear child?

RAINE   In Cornwall. With Patrice.

MARGARET   Oh. I see. And there weren't any friends, or
               relatives...

RAINE   Which way did you say... 237?

MARGARET   Large Sugar Maple–

MARGARET points in a direction – RAINE nods and turns to leave.

RAINE   Large Sugar Maple…

—— 5 ——

Lewis, Sparkle and Raine.

SPARKLE accompanies LEWIS on recorder.

LEWIS   *(in a comical hat singing for RAINE)* It's real… good to have ya, it's so… nice to meet ya, we heard so much about ya, so step right in. oh ya it's real… good… to have ya… it's so… nice… to meet ya… we heard SO much about you so step… right… in.

Hey. Cheer up. Elizabeth Raine McFurry McPhoo, because…

"you're with friendly people, who can't wait to know ya, ya look really special, you're gonna have a blast!" Eh? "You're with friendly people, who can't wait to know ya, ya look really special, and you're home at last. Oh yes, you're home… at… last!"

—— 6 ——

JANET   *(at her vanity, talks as if audience is mirror)* No, sugarplum, no that's only for big ladies; because it's very mucky it would muck up your beautiful lashes and it's very hard to get off BETHANY put it down. *(She calls to Hamish, offstage.)* Hamish!! will you please stop bouncing that ball love. *(Hamish enters.)* No! No I TOLD YOU this morning I was not going to give you money for a movie because of your rude behaviour – yes you were you were extremely rude, Hamey… to me AND to your father, yes, oh yes you were, about the lunch I made you, wasn't he Bethany? Hamey you threw it on the floor when you found out it was cream cheese and a bagel you threw it on the floor. AND you pushed Bethany last night, no, I am not giving you a cent.... Oh I'm just going across the street to Judy and Dave's, love, you know, with the four teenaged daughters? No, sorry, hon', I would adore to bring you but it's just a grown up thing. A very grown up thing; well we're talking about this GROUP home, remember you noticed the new teenagers bringing boxes into the Alexanders house? Well Mummy and the other people on the block are really happy that they are here, that you know, that they have a nice street to live on, because many of them come from troubled homes and places that don't look so nice, but some of the neighbours are QUITE concerned, and because I'm a lawyer, they wanted me to talk to them about... no, it's not that we don't like them, no, no of course they aren't bad guys, they're just sad teenagers, darling, it's just that we don't really know anything about them, and we think the man who bought the house should – no, it's not RACIST, Hamish, it's about property values for some of the neighbours and well, it means how much money our house is worth, and if they let their lawn go to weed, and the paint peel, and if they have big rave parties and make lots of noise and leave beer bottles... well, no, I don't actually think they will do that, I mean most of these homes work out just perfectly, so I am basically going to reassure everybody that it will be fine *just* fine and should be very nice to them.

(She puts it on.) That too much lipstick? Do I look pretty? Or like a clown? A clown? Thank YOU, Hamish.

You wonderful kids. Do you know I adore you both? Oh yes I do I more than – Okay, I'm sorry Hamish, I know you hate it when I say that. But you are you ARE my sweet sweet little boy the little boy who took big tantrums with your bright

red cheeks my little apple pie angel and you oh
yes, Bethany Bright I just I don't know I can't tell
you guys, Hamish just listen, please, I just... want
you to know.... Hamish stay here because I have
to tell you That I really really cherish you. LOVE
you LOFF am CRAZY about you I know you
know, of course you know, I mean mad crazy
WILD about you and I don't mean to embarrass
you... but I just feel like I could explode, like a
balloon that has more and more air every time
I look at you it's like God is blowing more more
adoration into me and I'm the balloon and there
is just more and more adoration and I'm getting
bigger and bigger and more and more see-
through and one day, one day I am just going
to – I'm a big balloon mother and if anyone in
any way hurts my children, that's you two I will
basically explode – in their faces. And the wind
from inside me will blow them blow them all
over and and will take their breath away. If they
hurt my children I will take their breath away.

—— 7 ——

RAINE and SPARKLE on steps.

SPARKLE Hullo.

RAINE doesn't answer.

You want to be left alone?

RAINE Yuh.

SPARKLE *(He hands her a sparkler, lights it.)* I'm named after
these. My dad brought em in after my mother
gave birth and she goes "Oh, there's a name."
Are you tripping?

RAINE A little.

SPARKLE Are you... sad?

RAINE   None of your business.

SPARKLE   OH. SoREE. You just look so MELancholy.

RAINE   Yeah. Well.

SPARKLE   Do you miss somebody?

RAINE   No.

SPARKLE   Are you far from home?

RAINE   No.

SPARKLE   Do you miss your home?

RAINE   I don't have a home to miss.

SPARKLE   Everybody comes from somewhere.

RAINE   No.

SPARKLE   Yes.

RAINE   No.

SPARKLE   Oh my goodness the air is green with your bitterness, girl. My grandmother used to say that.

RAINE   So.

SPARKLE   So. What are you gonna be for Halloween?

RAINE   Halloween?

SPARKLE   I know what I'm going to be. The Velveteen Rabbit. What do you think of that?

RAINE   Is your name really Sparkle?

SPARKLE   Is your name really Raine?

RAINE   You still go out for Halloween?

SPARKLE   So many windows to break, so much candy to
              steal so many eggs to throw I particularly like
              those little chewy wrapped caramel candies that
              take your teeth out, don't you? Don't you just
              love to to BITE into one of those and feel that you
              are...

RAINE   Would you please just leave me alone?

SPARKLE   You know, the first time I was in a group home I
              was six. I will never forget the feeling in my body
              when I crossed that threshold. As if all the breath
              in me escaped, and I was a flat plastic beachball.
              I felt that way for the whole six months.

RAINE   Six months?

              *RAINE shakes her head. Looks around. Sits down,
              very depressed. Lets her head hang down, between
              her knees.*

SPARKLE   Yeah. About six months.

RAINE   And then?

SPARKLE   And then? Well you're just not the same as you
              were, that's all. You're something different.

—— 8 ——

MARGARET calls for food.

MARGARET   Hello? Is this Mattucci's Food Market? Sam? Yes.
              Yes it's Margaret Deacon calling. Well yes, it has;
              oh yes, thank you I did receive your card and
              I very much appreciated it you will be getting
              a thank-you note... yes, yes,

              Well I am finally getting a bit of an appetite back,
              so I thought a half-a-pound of sliced – would you
              hold a minute Sam?

              JANET walks in, holding flowers.

–look – I'm terribly busy.

JANET I just… I really just wanted to say – I was really really really really sorry…

MARGARET Sam, I'll call you back with an order. *(hangs up phone)* What is that perfume you're wearing.

JANET Bethany poured it on me; Mummy, I just wanted to say–

MARGARET –Alright. You've said it. Goodbye now.

JANET Do you… forgive me, at all?

MARGARET I don't know.

JANET I really, just… I wanted to help you, Mum.

MARGARET Yes Janet. That is what you always say.

JANET And then I became King Kong, I know, it's unforgivable but Look. I promise. I won't… interfere any more, I just… want you to know… that I am – Your Daughter and you are My – Mother and I want only to–

MARGARET –Janet. Now, what do you think about this "home?"

JANET Well. I don't know. I think it'll be – fine, Mum. Michael and I both think it will be – fine. What do you think?

MARGARET I think we had better get our alarm systems working. Jim Nolan was telling me terrible stories about…

JANET Yeah. I suppose there is a… slim possibility–

MARGARET –Slim? Janet for heaven's sake wake up. My God. I really do not want to live the last ten or fifteen years of my life in fear. It's bad enough to fear my own body, and all the possibilities there, but to fear… thieves and rowdies, rapists!

JANET	Mum, I really don't think you need to be fearful…
MARGARET	Are you really that naive?
JANET	I'm hopeful, Mum, I–
MARGARET	Do you want your mother to live in fear, Janet? Do you want your children afraid to – walk on Mapleview Lanes?
JANET	No, of course not.
MARGARET	Then we must urge them to move somewhere else.
JANET	That would not be an easy thing, Mum. Really. It was clearly passed by the city, the Children's Aid… it would take a huge legal–
MARGARET	Well you're a lawyer, can't you do something about it?
JANET	No, no Mum I don't want to do something about it because, well, I believe in spite of our concerns, I believe it is their right to to – live on this–
MARGARET	Their right?
JANET	Um… yeah. Yes. Mummy. They do have to live somewhere.
MARGARET	Here. Take your flowers, for heaven's sake give them to someone who needs them.

MARGARET presses redial on her phone.

—— 9 ——

RAINE and LEWIS. Boom-box plays her favourite song.

LEWIS	Listen, just because you got the short end of the stick, and your mother passed when you were

only sixteen tender years old and your father is
a selfish shit does not mean that you are not
worthy. You understand that?

RAINE   Whatever.

LEWIS   Do you understand that?

RAINE   No.

LEWIS   RAINE.

RAINE   What.

LEWIS   I want you to – look up. I want you to look up at
that maple right there, towerin' over us, and the
light on the leaves my GOD and the shape of
those leaves, sharp and perfect, eh? and the
strong slim branches that is you, that is you and
the others and now cast those eyes of yours
downwards, right? And take a lookie at the trunk,
Raine. That trunk is the house, this house, strong
and firm holdin' all of you, my family, my girls
and boys, all of you up, and the roots? The roots
they go deep deep into the ground, right? And
they spread far and wide and they drink of the
groundwater the groundwater is the love we all
have for each other, eh? And – You – drink, girl,
you drink of that water, hear me? Because it is
here, flowin' strong from me to you, and it is not
gonna stop so drink drink and drink.

———— 10 ————

On the phone.

MARGARET   Hello, John. Yes, yes it's Margaret. Well thank
you, yes, it has been a long time, I'm afraid I have
been rather reclusive since Ian's death oh well
I thought so too. Oh he was very fond of you, too,
uh huh. Look John, I was just calling about the
Weeping Willow we share, well about the broken
branch – Oh… good GOOD And what about this

– Oh well I'm glad you said that, John, I couldn't agree with you more; oh yes, I KNOW Ian would have been outraged.

—— 11 ——

SPARKLE and RAINE.

Late at night. RAINE asleep. SPARKLE appears breathless. He opens his backpack.

SPARKLE   You were playing Nintendo with me all night, okay? We were playing "Dark Rhapsody" and I fell asleep, and you were like watching me sleep...

RAINE   What's going on?

          SPARKLE opens the sack and spills the contents in front of her.

SPARKLE   BOUNTY, beautiful bounty.

RAINE   What's this?

SPARKLE   Number 459. It was so obvious they're away, blinds down, newspapers piling up, desperate cat rubbing against my leg.

RAINE   How'd you get in?

SPARKLE   Through the mailbox, I'm a shapeshifter.

RAINE   Sparkle. You BROKE into a HOUSE?

SPARKLE   Look! A silver fork! An actual sterling silver fork! And a knife! and a spoon and two five-dollar bills and even, even, a teenaged girly girls diary!!! "my mother is so incredibly lame she was wearing knee socks today. I ate two chocolate bars yesterday I am getting so fat Fat fat fat I hate myself." I could get THOUSANDS for this!! I could go on Antiques Road show and and...

RAINE I can't believe you broke into a house...

SPARKLE I know, it's so immature. In fact it's babyish. It was so clean the floors smelled like bleach. And they had like sixteen different kinds of crackers, just crazy about crackers I guess, and...

RAINE That's exactly what they expect us to do, Sparkle. Why are you playing into their worst...?

SPARKLE Because. It's exciting. To go where you aren't supposed to go. To go where you would never EVER be invited. I didn't steal anything expensive, I didn't touch the Rolex watch, or the jewellry, or the new IMAX computer, or the fancy pantsy ART OR the Siamese CAT.

RAINE You are so Weird.

SPARKLE Gonna turn me in?

RAINE ...no

SPARKLE Because I would drown myself in the sink before I go back to jail.

RAINE Don't worry.

SPARKLE Harry and Doreen are RUTHLESS with squealers, you should have SEEN what they did to little DAVID over at Parkdale? Drove him out to the zoo in the middle of the night, and threw him in naked with the Siberian tigers, I am serious, the tiger mauled him almost to death he only has one hand now it was all over the news – they are really rough people, though, don't you find? Have you watched the way Doreen eats?

RAINE Everytime we're in the same room she says "what are you looking at?" I don't think she likes me.

SPARKLE She hates you, she told me.

RAINE Promise me you won't do that again.

SPARKLE   HAH! You're really hilarious you know that?
           I mean really really, side splittingly hi-larious!!
           HA HA HA HA HAHAHAH!!

RAINE   Sparkle! It could be very bad for Lewis. With the
           neighbours and everything. Very VERY bad.
           Lewis would be VERY mad at you, you know.

SPARKLE   Ohhhhh "Lewwwisss" is it? It's so obvious you
           have a big wonking crush on him, the way your
           voice sort of wavers when you say his name.

RAINE   Mr. Chance? Are you kidding me?

SPARKLE   It's okay, everyone has a crush on him.

RAINE   Well I don't. I think he's an asshole.

SPARKLE   YEAH? If you think he's such an asshole why do
           you STARE at him?

RAINE   I stare at Mr. Chance?

SPARKLE   You can't take your eyes OFFA him. Anyway
           darling, he's taken.

RAINE   He's married?

SPARKLE   (*laughs, hard*) HAHAH! I think he was, actually, to
           some shopgirl from New Brunswick with too
           much lip liner and a name like Sherry Lynn when
           he was like in HIGH school. But not NOW silly.
           Now he has a boyfriend.

RAINE   He's gay.

SPARKLE   Well duh. DOZY HEAD. DUH–

RAINE   Why are you being – so–

SPARKLE   He doesn't like girls. Is that clear?

RAINE   Sparkle. I am not in the LEAST interested in Mr.
           Chance. It has never OCCURRED to me, actually,
           and I resent you implying that I…

SPARKLE   Yakety yakety yakety yak. You TALK too much,
              girlfriend.

              He smokes.

RAINE   I think you're the one with the crush on Mr.
              Chance.

SPARKLE   Who me? Please. He is totally not my type. He
              is SO lower middle. I mean his shoes? Did you
              happen to notice his shoes?

RAINE   I still think you have a crush on him.

              Scene overlap.

MARGARET   –Excuse Me–

———— 12 ————

              MARGARET at night in her nightgown.

MARGARET   *(shouting out the back window)* –Hello? Hello!!
              Would you mind please not having your gather-
              ing on my property? I know that is pot you are
              smoking I lived through the sixties remember and
              I can't and won't stoop to pick up your cigarette
              ends. Oh my goodness. There is no need to be so
              rude that language may be acceptable where you
              come from but it is not acceptable on Mapleview
              Lanes! Now get off my property or I'm calling the
              police!

———— 13 ————

              *LEWIS is in a hyper and fun mood; he is blowing
              his lips like a horse. He moves like a horse.
              SPARKLE knows the game. They include RAINE.*

SPARKLE   Horse!! You're a horse!! Okay now ME.

              SPARKLE does a very good cat.

LEWIS	What's new, Pussy cat, WHA A A A A What's new, pussycat…
SPARKLE	YES! You GOT IT! OH my GOD you got it!! *(He hugs LEWIS and RAINE.)* Rainey? Rainey you go now.
RAINE	Ahhh…

RAINE does an odd rabbit. They are both puzzled.

Come on you guys, it's obvious!

LEWIS	A worm? A bird! Like one of those, like peace birds, whaddya call em?
SPARKLE	DOVES! Is it a dove?
RAINE	It's a RABBIT, you Dodoes! See? Look!
SPARKLE	Of course. IT is SO a rabbit.
RAINE	*(to LEWIS)* See Mr. Chance?
LEWIS	Of course I do I lost my mind because horses, of courses, think like horses okay, rabbit, and pussy-cat, get on the horse, I'm a wild horse, see, and we're gonna race, race to the desert… *(He sings the William Tell tune. His cell phone goes off.)* …ahhhh a rattlesnake, I'm throwin you off, sorry guys, hold on, I'm neighhhhhhhhh neighhhhhhhh…

They fall off laughing.

Gotta go see ya later, don't forget Sparks, your turn to make supper!

—— **14** ——

SPARKLE undoes his buttons, one by one.

SPARKLE	…He loves me He loves me not He loves me He loves me not. He loves me…. Yo Rabbit, you still

haven't told me why you are here, why are you here?

RAINE   My mother died – HAH!

SPARKLE   That sucks.

RAINE   Father's a dick.

SPARKLE   Goes without saying.

RAINE   Kicked out of my friends zero relatives, so! Why are you here?

SPARKLE   Oh, me? I'm unmanageable.

RAINE   What does that mean, unmanageable?

SPARKLE   Oh, nothing really. Just… I killed my parents.

RAINE   You did not.

SPARKLE   Oh yes. I did. And I had my reasons.

RAINE   Really? Honestly?

SPARKLE   I had… my… reasons. And that's why I'm here. Nobody wants to adopt somebody who killed his parents, right?

       RAINE is not sure. SPARKLE laughs.

       —— 15 ——

       LEWIS is at his desk on the telephone. He is drinking.

LEWIS   Hello, Ma? S'Lewis. Did I wake ya? I know you said you watch "Biography" from 1-2 so I figured you'd be up for another 5 minutes. Who they doin'? Audrey Hepburn, she was somethin special, eh? Yah. Oh fine, how are you? Good, excellent. Just in the air, here, over Iceland, no I'm

home, doin' the bills, I wish I was in the air; goin'
somewhere warm; yah it's goin' pretty good, the
house is somethin, Ma, oh you're gonna love it
and the kids are just great, really nice bunch; oh
terrible lives, yah, oh mostly neglect you know?
Parents in their party years. Some things you
wouldn't want to know… oh no, I'll never tell,
you know me yeah… oh yeah… the neighbours
are givin me grief of course oh my God letters,
calls, cuttin me dead when I say hello on the
street so you know, that's a laugh.

I was just thinking. I was thinking about William.
Yeah. He comes into my head. And there he is,
you know, his face, in the snowstorm, when I was
checkin on him and he's inside my coat and the
wind is blowin the bejeesus out my face and
I look at his face and–

—— 16 ——

*MARGARET in a park, in the middle of night,
very dark. Meets RAINE.*

RAINE   Hello? Excuse me. Aren't you…?

MARGARET   Oh Hello Raine. Yes, it's me, Margaret… I was
           just taking my midnight walk. I sometimes see
           rabbits in this park, the occasional fox. Once I
           even saw a flash of Ian, my late husband, behind
           the hawthorne tree. I really did see him standing
           there, with a mug of tea, half smiling at me. Don't
           tell anyone I said that. I have been hoping to see
           you.

RAINE   How are you? Are you okay?

MARGARET   Yes. Yes, I'm feeling… somewhat brighter. Since
           you came.

RAINE   Really?

MARGARET   I ordered pizza.

RAINE	That's great.
MARGARET	I've even picked up a few things. Tell me. Are you liking your... new... residence?
	RAINE shakes her head.
	Poor dear. You're missing your mother aren't you?
RAINE	No.
MARGARET	Yes.
RAINE	No. Not at all, I don't even dream about her, it's just–
MARGARET	It's not what you are accustomed to, is it?
RAINE	THE SMELL!
MARGARET	Look at you, you're in the same trousers and pullover – it's sinful! Your shoes are... scuffed. Have they not given you a clothing fund, or...
RAINE	NOPE.
MARGARET	Appalling! That man gets an enormous sum of money for each and every one of you.
RAINE	Really?
MARGARET	Oh yes YES. More than two hundred dollars a day is what my friend in the ministry said.
RAINE	No way! 200 dollars a day for each and every one of us?
MARGARET	12 Children; That's more than 16 thousand a week my dear.
RAINE	No, that couldn't be right. She's just – your friend has got it wrong.

MARGARET   I don't think so. Oh Raine you don't look happy
           at all.

RAINE   They're really – like – rough, you know?

MARGARET   But you don't belong there.

RAINE   I don't really sleep…. But but but the thing is
           I love being *here*, though. You know? On this
           street. With all the big maple trees, I like… walk-
           ing around the block. It reminds me… of where
           I grew up.

MARGARET   I planted that crabapple myself. Would you…
           just… sit with me for a moment?

RAINE   Sure.

           MARGARET holds RAINE's hand.

MARGARET   Do you mind? I haven't held my own daughter's
           hand since she was six years old.

RAINE   Why not?

MARGARET   I don't know.

RAINE   I never held my mother's hand either.

MARGARET   And why…

RAINE   I'm not sure…

MARGARET   You have cold hands, like me.

RAINE   Yeah. My hands and feet, always cold.

MARGARET   Me too.

RAINE   Feels like it could snow tonight. I hope it snows.

MARGARET   I ordered in some gooey biscuits for you, I hope
           you'll come and see me and I've made Popsicles
           from some apple juice I found in the cupboard,

	my grandchildren LOVE them. *(beat)* Poor Raine…
RAINE	…One girl… she burns her arms with cigarettes… this other one screams all night, there's a guy who punches holes in the wall and another one says he killed his parents.
MARGARET	Good God. You shouldn't be in there a day longer, listen, I will do my best to make arrangements for you–
RAINE	No, no please – I like it there, I hate it there but I like it there. I mean–

—— 17 ——

RAINE and SPARKLE on Mapleview.

SPARKLE	What is the name of this street anyway? It's like something out of fucking Pleasantville.
RAINE	Mapleview Lanes…
SPARKLE	*(laughs hysterically)* That's hilarious! MAPLEVIEW LANES!! AGHHHHH! I love it. I just LOVE those NAMES of any development built from the six-ties on? Like ahhh "Fairfield Estates" or Winchester Woods or or Birchmeadow Crescent All EXCLUSIVE LIFESTYLE LIVING ExCLUDING the likes of US, right?
RAINE	Sparkle. You changed the subject.
SPARKLE	I know, let's colour our hair.
RAINE	SPARKLE. Come on. Let's do it. Let's find out the truth about the money, don't you want to know if he's ripping us off?

SPARKLE grabs her tightly.

SPARKLE   I LOVE the man, Raine, you don't seem to understand…. I mean for me we're living LUXURY
I mean compared to what I grew up with? HAH!
When Carla would like cook something in the
oven? Like a frozen pizza? You could hear the
cockroaches exploding there was mice shit all
over the counter every morning the toilet never
worked, it was city housing, right? There was no
heat there were holes in the wall; Dad used to
drag my mother by the hair and put her hand on
the burner sometimes he got so bad we would all
hide up on the roof? The five of us he never
thought to look there and we would be there
huddled under blankets it was really fun actually
one night the Social Worker Karen walked in?
And then we all got removed and Carla wept.
She sat on the roof and wept I will never forget
the sight of her…

RAINE   Oh Sparkle, that's awful–

SPARKLE   Would be if it were true, huh?

RAINE is puzzled, SPARKLE laughs and laughs.

—— 18 ——

MARGARET on the phone with Laurel.

MARGARET   Laurel? Yes, it's Margaret Deacon here again.
Listen, I've been thinking about your idea of me
taking Trish Van Gelder's place in the book club.
Well I've started reading the most marvellous
book It's a sort of biography of Suzannah
Moodie.

Yes.

I heard the place was ransacked; terrible. Oh yes
we must take action "action starts now," who said
that, wasn't it Winston Churchill?

Yes, well that's grand I'll bring my mushroom
pate.

—— **19** ——

LEWIS holds a letter he has just read in his hand;
it is another resident's letter protesting the house.

LEWIS — I'm afraid this time, you know that? I'm afraid we might lose this one.

SPARKLE — No, no way, you always win.

LEWIS — These people are different. They got bigger guns, you know. Deeper pockets.

SPARKLE — You smell so nice. Like the dock, you know? Sort of Lake Ontario, and gasoline, and old wood and – what...

LEWIS is uncomfortable with that kind of talk.
He is reading a residents letter referring to the
break-in.

LEWIS — Are you SURE you didn't have anything to do with that B & E down the street? Because if you did so help me God I'll...

SPARKLE — Oh please You really think I want the pain in the ass of selling a hot PC or some old lady silver? That's for twelve-year-olds, Lewis. I've graduated far beyond simple B & E's.

LEWIS — They all think its one of you, of course.

SPARKLE — You look like a train wreck, by the way, are you alright?

LEWIS — I just don't know if I have the energy this time. I'm tired, Spark. I'm gettin' old. My back is givin out on me. Feel like an old man.

SPARKLE — Do I hear you say you are giving up?

LEWIS — You heard me say I was tired. Get outa here. I'm busy.

SPARKLE	You'll never give up. You're made for war, Lew.
LEWIS	Oh. Is that what I'm made for?
SPARKLE	Oh yeah. YAH! It's that IRA blood you have running through those veins of yours. Weren't you tellin' me your grandfather got shot in Bloody Sunday or somethin'? Men of courage are SO SEXY. YOU are so sexy.
LEWIS	Listen to me.
SPARKLE	What.
LEWIS	You know what.
SPARKLE	What?
LEWIS	I've told you. I find that talk inappropriate. Entirely completely inappropriate. So don't... talk like that. Anymore. Now leave me, go watch cartoons. I have work to do.
SPARKLE	You like me. I know you do.
LEWIS	Sparks back off. Enough of that.
SPARKLE	You look at me. I've seen you looking at me.
LEWIS	(*LEWIS moves away from SPARKLE.*) You've seen what you want to see, Sparks. Now get out.
SPARKLE	With the *hungriest* eyes I have ever.
LEWIS	Darlene? Amir? Will you come in here for a minute please.
SPARKLE	WAIT. I'm sorry. I won't anymore. I was just teasing, Lewis. I PROMISE. Please.
LEWIS	Look. I'm tellin' you I'm gonna lose this house and you think it's some kinda goddamn game, Sparkle. Will you wake up? WILL YA WAKE UP?

SPARKLE   What do you want from me? I'm a kid, I'm only
             18 and a half years old like WHAT do you
             WANT?

LEWIS   I want... you... to GIVE a shit. You've been livin
             with us for four years now, we've given you love
             we've given you food we've given you comfort
             I WANT you to CARE! Is there ANYTHING in
             this WORLD you CARE about?

—— 20 ——

MARGARET and JANET eating take-out.

MARGARET   You don't seem to have done ANYTHING aside
             from that USELESS petition that's limping around
             the block!

JANET   The mango salad is wonderful Mum, why don't
             you try some? You love mango.

MARGARET   What about John Pritchard's lawsuit idea?

JANET   It's not spicy at all, here – I made sure of that. I
             said "no spices..."

MARGARET   Janet we have a crisis here.

JANET   Mum. Why don't you ever look at me when you
             speak to me? Is there something about my face?

MARGARET   Oh good heavens Janet why must everything be
             about you.

JANET   You make me feel... well, really, kind of invisible.

MARGARET   Are you going to divert this conversation into a
             psychodrama?

JANET   No. I don't have time to do that, Mum, I have a
             meeting with our most important corporate client
             in forty-five minutes, I just want to know, quickly,

just for the heck of it, why don't you ever look at me?

MARGARET   Oh Good Lord – what NEXT? You have ALWAYS pestered me, ever since you were a little girl tugging at my coat "Mummy, look at me, Mummy, Mummy!"

JANET   "Pestered." That is a really NASTY word to use, mother.

MARGARET   It is a nasty thing to DO.

JANET   Oh my God. Oh. My. God. I'm sorry. I have pestered you. *(Silent beat, she breaks down.)* I don't know why I'm so– *(MARGARET comforts her reluctantly.)* How can I – how can I ever... make it up to you?

MARGARET strokes her daughter's hair.

MARGARET   By making this neighbourhood – safe for Bethany and Hamish, for your beautiful children; and for me;

JANET pulls away.

By waking up from your bleeding-heart stupor and and helping us!

Or are we the ones who are invisible to you?

—— 21 ——

RAINE is going through papers. LEWIS walks in.

LEWIS   Hullo there, Rainers. What can I help you with?

RAINE   Oh. Just... I was just looking for my health card.

LEWIS   How did you get in here? I believe it was locked when I left.

RAINE	No it wasn't. I just opened it.
LEWIS	I believe it was locked.
RAINE	No.
LEWIS	You know this is a private office, Raine. I don't allow anyone in here when I'm not here. There is restricted information in here.
RAINE	Okay. I'm sorry I just feel really really sick and I wanted to go to that clinic. You have no idea how sick I feel.
LEWIS	Fine. I'll get the card for you. All you had to do was ask. *(He searches.)*
RAINE	No.
LEWIS	What.
RAINE	I lied.
LEWIS	Yes.
RAINE	I want to know how much.
LEWIS	How much what?
RAINE	How much money you get for each of us.
LEWIS	WHAT?
RAINE	I want to know how much you get for each of us. I think that's my right.
LEWIS	Raine. Honey. That's confidential.
RAINE	THAT is bullshit.
LEWIS	Raine. I am not about to go through all my accounting with a child.
RAINE	A CHILD?

LEWIS   Yes, frankly.

RAINE   Mr. Chance tell me something. Why do you run this group home? Isn't it because the government gives you thousands of dollars every month for each of us? Isn't it?

LEWIS   Do you want to know why I do this, Raine?

RAINE   I know why you do this.

LEWIS   He was the tenth, the last child, right? He was a real surprise to my Mum she was goin' on forty-seven, eh? But the pregnancy was fine, and she had him in two hours, And when I walked into that hospital room and saw that little baby boy wrapped in a blue blanket lyin there in my mother's arms I was so high, I'm tellin you. I loved my sisters, but after eight of them I have to admit I had been longing for a boy. A baby brother to throw around a ball with, you know. I was though the roof. We were all pretty happy, right? Pretty jazzed. And William? He just slept and slept and when he was awake? He smiled. And smart? Oh you knew he was smart the way he watched things. Those little brown eyes, just watchin' the world. I would sit and stare at him, for hours, just talk to him, about my day, about his day, I would tell him stories about each of his sisters. He liked that. I don't know, William? He just made the whole world seem right.

As RAINE listens, she is taken back to her own brush with death in infancy.

Then around Christmas time, William got sick.

At first it was a good thing, that William was sick, you know, sleepin all the time. I was thinkin Hey, this virus is okay, the baby is even easier than before, I can get so much done, you know, while Mum is busy cleanin all those fine Fredericton Houses on the River; Well on the Sunday right before Christmas, we were all in the house under

Stephen
Ouimette
as LEWIS,
Holly
Lewis
as RAINE.

photo by
David
Hawe.

the blankets wrapping little presents that my
Mum had been keeping all year, things the rich
people had put in the garbage, and it got to be
about two o'clock in the afternoon and I suddenly
realized William still wasn't up I asked Mum
where was William and she said "still sleeping he
had a hard night" but I felt uneasy somehow so
I ran up and I looked in his crib and he was
sleeping, but he was breathin way too fast, eh,
I never heard such fast breathing, and there was
this rasping every time he breathed, I didn't like
it all. I picked him up and brought him down to
Mum, and I go "Mum, is it normal for him to be
breathin' so fast? Well she looked at the clock and
she counted. Seventy-two breaths in one minute.
Well we looked at each other and she said
"Lewis, we gotta take William to hospital, He has
pneumonia." Well the trouble was, we were about
six miles out in the country, right? And we had
no car. And the neighbours, Lorraine and John,
they were not home. They were all down the
Mirimichi visiting her mother they were not
comin home for hours and hours if at all. And
there was no one else on the other side. Just a
deserted farm house. Mum and I looked outside,
it was comin on to a snowstorm and she goes
"One of us is going to have to take him. And my
feet are hurtin so much, Lewis, I can hardly walk.
If you start walkin with him now you could be
there by supper time. And the minute Lorraine
and John pull up I'll get em to run me in."

Well, nobody is gonna bring those snow
machines out to where we were livin. So there
I am with baby William under my coat, walking,
the wind just tearin through me, walkin six miles
and the snow keeps falling and the baby, his
breathin, so loud, so fast so fast I finally get into
Fredericton after a couple of hours I walk up the
big long hill to the hospital feels like it's taking
forever you know and then there I am, at the hospital. And I walk in with William in my coat,
breathin, breathin so fast, now lighter though,
can't hear the breathing so well now, and they

make me sit in the waiting room with William, I
shout at em, "this is a sick baby we got here,
"he's breathin seventy-two times in minute" but
they don't listen we sit there for three hours that
night, and when this young Chinese doctor finally saw William he goes "this is a sick baby" and
he admits William, and tells me I can go. I tell
them I am not going anywhere I will be waitin in
the waitin room all night if I had to and would
they please come and tell me how he was doin
but they aren't payin no attention to me, they are
puttin needles and lines and and even a breathing
tube into poor William, who looks like like a
small cloud how if you were to touch it it would
kind of disappear around you that is what
I thought–

Well, Raine, I'm not going to bore you with the
rest of it, me comin in and out, the security kickin
me out William bein taken to the ICU my mother
runnin through the hospital walkin into the room
and passin out when she saw William. I will just
tell you what you already know is that William
did not survive the night. The neighbours did not
get back till two in the morning and by the time
my mother got to the hospital, just before two-
thirty he was gone.

When she came to she was silent for a very very
long time. Then she looked at him and touched
his forehead, and she said "I guess he knew he
was one too many." They were waiting for her to
cry. But she didn't cry. That was not my mother.

So why I'm tellin you all this is, I always felt,
somehow that I had let William die. That if I had
only had the sense to go into the first house I saw
and call an ambulance, or if I had walked faster,
or gone upstairs at one instead of two that afternoon, or shouted down the emergency waiting
room until they looked at William that things
woulda turned out different. And because I felt
I had failed my baby brother I vowed; I VOWED
to give my life to the children we have all failed.

I said to myself I am going to bring them into a house like the houses my mother cleaned every day of her life roomy airy, and full of light. I'm going to bring them into this house and I'm going to say "this is your home." THIS IS YOUR HOME.

And tell me. Do you honestly think I would bring you into my home and I would... in any way...

They embrace.

ACT TWO

—— 1 ——

> *JANET and MARGARET call on LEWIS. They*
> *begin by shaking hands.*

JANET & LEWIS	Hi!
JANET	Janet Grant.
MARGARET	Margaret Deacon.
LEWIS	Really good to meet you both! Lewis Chance, as you probably know. *(to JANET)* Hey, I saw those chocolate brown eyes of yours at the big meetin', didn't I?
JANET	Oh yes, I was there!
LEWIS	And you, you must be her baby sister, right?
MARGARET	Oh dear.
JANET	That was a great speech you gave. Mum, you would have been very impressed, Mr. Chance is a very good speaker.
LEWIS	Excellent. So what can I do for you ladies today? I know you're not here to sell me carpet cleaning.
JANET	No. I need carpet cleaning actually. My dog, she runs through the mud… and…
LEWIS	Number 389. The fieldstone. With the weeping willow in front, S'beautiful. You have a beautiful home.
JANET	Oh, well thank you, we like it.
MARGARET	So. Shall we get down to business?

LEWIS   And you... are at 207 – Rainers told me all about
               you, she's nuts about you.

MARGARET   Well I'm very fond of her.

LEWIS   ...SO.

MARGARET   Mr. Lewis. We want you to know right now that
               we, the residents of Mapleview Lanes frankly
               oppose–

JANET   Mum. Please. That's not true at all, it's just.... We
               are really here on a kind of... well a fact-finding
               mission some of us, there are just a few things we
               want... we need to know... about... the home...
               and...

LEWIS   Uh huh. Sure. What do you want to know?

MARGARET   Everything, Mr.–

LEWIS   CHANCE.

JANET   Your letters have been VERY helpful, but there
               are... we do have some concerns, of course, I am
               sure you've run into this before, irate residents,
               well that is not us, we are very progressive
               people generally but... there are some concerns.

MARGARET   MANY URGENT concerns.

JANET   Mum.

LEWIS   Sure.... And I want you to know I appreciate
               your coming today. You are the only people in the
               neighbourhood who have bothered to ring the
               doorbell, to see the place, to actually talk to me
               like a human being.

JANET   Well thank you. For saying that. I hate the whole
               "my lawyer will talk to your lawyer," although
               I am a lawyer, (She laughs, hard and a bit forced.)
               but I'm not here as a lawyer.

LEWIS	No?
JANET	Oh no.
MARGARET	Well, Janet…
JANET	No! God no, Mum. Please. Just… as a neighbour. Who who… I think it is wonderful that you have given these kids a home, and I truly think it is our responsibility as citizens to to… welcome them. But I also do think that it is our right–
LEWIS	Your right?
MARGARET	Yes our right.
JANET	Our right to know. More about our new neighbours. Mr. Chance this neighbourhood, Mapleview Lanes is our WORLD I grew up here, there is a way of life here, a routine, certain sounds and sights we are accustomed to, and you know what I mean, you grew up in a small place, wasn't it Herring Cove in in New Brunswick, that was your world.
LEWIS	That. was. my. world.
JANET	And your neighbourhood, was everything to you, I am sure. I know that you KNOW, understand how deeply felt…
LEWIS	VERY deeply felt.
MARGARET	I must say I do not care for your tone Mr. Chance.
JANET	Mum, please; I'm sorry my Mother is…
MARGARET	Janet.
LEWIS	HAH. I've always been a sucker for a mother-daughter act. NOW. Let's be honest.
MARGARET	We are ALWAYS honest, Mr. Chance.

LEWIS	You are not just here as neighbours, you are here on behalf of the neighbours, the IRATE neighbours you spoke of, the well-connected, rich, and pissed off.
JANET	Well it is really not so formal as that, I just volunteered to come and ask you a few questions really–
MARGARET	I wouldn't describe any of us as RICH–
JANET	–We are HERE, Mr. Chance,
LEWIS	And you are armed and dangerous, eh! I'll say; I received your letter lady, words like bullets every one. VERY impressive. Where'd you learn how to write like that, Janet?
JANET	Oh well I really didn't mean it to sound threatening, that's just legalese–
LEWIS	HAH; THAT'S who you remind me of! Sister Mary Terese my ENGLISH teacher that woman kicked the shit outa me so many times sorry, I do apologize for my vulgar language, but you know, a boy from Herring Cove!! (*JANET pulls a paper out.*) So what's that you got there, Mrs. Grant.... Don't tell me, let me guess.... It's... a... petition...!!! Hey, I figured, some go-getter was gonna come up with one of these boys. I started a petition once. When I was a kid. It was for them to bring back "Gilligan's Island," I loved that show, Didn't do a damn thing. So this is yours. YOUR petition. To have... don't tell me let me guess... the house closed!

Lewis grabs the petition.

JANET	Oh no, no GOD no, it's it's just a – a sort of covenant.
LEWIS	Oh HEY, hold the ladder steady you did WELL, you got a shitload of names here.

JANET	Just about everyone–
LEWIS	GOOD GIRL. Your Mom's gonna be proud of You. You want your Mama to be proud of you, don't you? Whewhoo! You have em hogtied eh?
JANET	WHAT?
LEWIS	SIGN or be SLAUGHTERED. You know what I'm talkin' about. Maybe they are old, and frail, and they need the support of their neighbours. Or new to the city and in need of friends. And if you turn against them, the whole block turns against them, because you and your mother are bosses of the block, now aren't you Mrs. Grant.
JANET	Oh my God. I've never heard anything more ridiculous.
LEWIS	Girl, I have been through this twenty times. And every time there is someone like the two of you, bosses of the block, got everybody quaking in their boots, no damn different than the play-ground. And you are the bully shovin the kids and me off the monkey bars. And the others, they're all too scared to lose their place on the bars, eh? So they are just hanging there, tremblin hoping you won't notice them, ya bullies! You low down ugly and immoral bullies. You oughta be ashamed of yourselves.

Margaret goes to speak.

You know what you can do with this petition, don't ya? You can take this petition and you can stick it up your ARSE!

Margaret turns away, trembling.

MARGARET	Good Lord.

Lewis whistles and laughs.

LEWIS	Just stick it where the sun don't never shine, honey.
JANET	Mr. Chance please, my mother is not accus-tomed–
MARGARET	People may speak that way to each other in Herring Cove, but around here, we believe in–
LEWIS	Fuck you you old bag of shit.
MARGARET	I'm leaving Janet. I need to take my heart medication.
JANET	Oh I'll– *(She dashes with the intent to accompany her Mother.)*
MARGARET	No Janet, You stay and you say what needs to be said. You tell him about our intention to file a lawsuit. You tell him EVERYTHING.

Margaret leaves in a flourish.

LEWIS	LAWSUIT LAWSUIT? Whew!! You people are hunting bear, aren't ya? AREN'T YA NOW?
JANET	Listen to me. I came here to ask you some ques-tions and I am going to ask them. Number One: Are any of these children young offenders?
LEWIS	Not at present they're not.
JANET	What I mean is have any of them ever been young offenders?
LEWIS	Oh I am not at liberty to tell you that, Miss Grant.
JANET	I think it is your ethical responsibility to tell me that Mr. Chance.
LEWIS	It is my ethical responsibility to protect the privacy of my wards, Janet. Even if I KNEW Ms Grant, which I do not, I would never, even on PAIN of DEATH, tell you.

JANET	Mr. Chance, surely you can understand what I am asking you...
LEWIS	I cannot answer.
JANET	Human to human Mr. Chance...
LEWIS	Human to human, I am not obliged to answer you.

JANET loudly exhales.

JANET	Listen. We could HELP you find another house.
LEWIS	What?
JANET	Sally Pritchard is a TOP real estate agent she has some WONDERFUL ideas. Look I have several...
LEWIS	Get out of here.
JANET	We could get the children into special programs at the school, we could arrange mentors, tutors... this is just NOT a good street for...
LEWIS	Go take a shit somewhere. (*She turns, shocked.*)
JANET	WHAT?
LEWIS	You heard me.
JANET	Uhhh. You are even worse than I thought.
LEWIS	MUCH worse.
JANET	My mother was right about you. She was SO right, she spotted you for a con artist right away. Your total disregard for the sensitivities of the neighbours, your disgusting brutality towards me and my mother, your–
LEWIS	This is my house. I paid for it. And what happens inside it is NONE of your BUSINESS. I don't have to answer to you for ANYTHING.

JANET   Listen, you parasite IF one of your kids breaks
         into one of our houses and murders one of us, do
         you answer for that?

LEWIS   Sure. Why not, baby?

JANET   You are going to be exposed, Mr. Chance for the
         lowlife you are, your pose as the defender of the
         children is going to collapse when we start dig-
         ging into your life. We have FOUR lawyers on
         this block, we have a bank president, we have the
         Dean of medicine.... And yes there will be a law-
         suit, Mr. Chance and we will CHASE you out of
         here–

LEWIS   I believe in these children. I believe in their right
         to live in your neighbourhood. I believe in *their*
         right to call it their neighbourhood. And whatev-
         er you think of me, I will fight to the death, for
         their rights. (*He tears up the petition.*) So you can
         get your bony ass out of that chair and walk on
         out of here. You can go to city hall, you can reach
         into your deep pockets and file a big fat lawsuit
         but you are going to lose girl, you and your nasty
         little schoolyard bully friends are going to be
         sprawled on the dirt wailing because we are here
         to stay. Now get out of my house!

         She leaves. He spits at her.

         *RAINE and SPARKLE have been listening They
         watch JANET, furious, steam out of the house and
         away. Then they hear LEWIS yell from inside.*

         —— 2 ——

         *RAINE and SPARKLE watch JANET leave, and
         share a joint. Pause.*

RAINE   My Dad is Jewish, (*or any non-White ethnicity*) you
         know? And when he was a kid? His family
         moved onto this WASPY street somewhere in
         Rosedale, right? And he remembers being *stoned*

by the neighbourhood kids. Every day. He
remembers that there was a petition to to force
his family off the street. But they fought it
Sparkle, they didn't just LEAVE you can't do
what they–

They start to giggle.

SPARKLE   Y'know what? You have a moustache. I wasn't
gonna tell you but in certain lights you look like a
15-year-old boy or something, you REALLY
should do something about it.

SPARKLE exits.

—— 3 ——

LEWIS in his comfortable chair; calls his mother.

LEWIS   Hey Carrie, it's Lewis here, yes, you're uncle
Lewis. How ya doin' beautiful? Yah? Yah! What
colour? Red, oh I love red toenails will you paint
mine when I come at Christmas? Excellent. Hey,
is your grandma there?

Ma? S'me Lewis. Is this a bad time? I could call
back later. oh okay. Good. So how ya doin? Yeah?
Did you change that medication? I know it was
makin' your heart skip, did you tell Dr. Day?
Well he's an idiot, Mum, look, when I come home
at Christmas I'm takin' you into Moncton and
we're gonna see somebody new. Uh huh. Well he
doesn't even have to know, Mum. She is, no way,
she say that? What'd she say? Mrs. Berkeley said
that? Oh you don't have to take that, Mum, tell
her to shove it; I know, but Mum just because
she's a doctor's wife does not mean she can talk
to you that way. Why should you go on your
hands and knees for her, you have more money
than she does anyway oh yes you Do Mum, I told
you its sittin' in that account just waiting for you
to – no, ANYTIME you want. You do not have to
take that, Mum, that is what I been trying to tell

you no, no that Money is for you to do whatever
you want with its for you to spend Ma, Mum,
Mum. Okay. We'll talk about it when I get there.
No no way I'm not givin' Mike a penny I told
him that before Uh huh. no, you just… yeah.
Yeah. Oh well, sure, they're puttin up a fight, as
usual. Only they got bigger weapons this time, if
you know what I mean? Oh yeah, well it is kinda
gettin' to me, Mum. You know they're draggin'
me to this big showdown at city hall next week,
Oh yeah, it'll be like Battle of… I don't know
what… I'm havin' trouble sleepin'. I keep thinkin'
about you-know-who. Yeah. Yeah his face, you
know? Like it was like he was lookin' at me with
this trust that I would do something, right? I
know, I know, but that's what I see, right. So I
was wondering, weren't you tellin' me something
about some tea or somethin' that knocked you
right out when you were up nights worryin'
about Maureen? Cam-o-mile. Right, right, I seen
that. With a couple of Gravol ground in okay, I'm
doin that tonight. I'm telling you it's – Yeah.
Listen. I wanted to ask you. Have you ever, had
like an enemy?

— 4 —

JANET with a Scotch and soda.

JANET (*on cell phone*) Oh awful, AWFUL the man is a
gangster Michael, mother is completely right; the
things he SAID to me; I don't know, after that I'm
kinda thinking Mum and her friends have a
point, you know, no, I'm still all FOR the poor
street kids – oh yes, but I am SO going to join the
fight against the bastard. No of course it's nothing to DO with being afraid of her, Michael,
I agree with her now, that's all. God. Michael
somebody has to fight for our neighbourhood,
protect it from the THUGS of the world – listen it
is my JOB to protect my children isn't it? I mean
tell me something, would a lioness just lie around
and and… (*She drops the phone.*)

—— 5 ——

Middle of the night. Outside. LEWIS is smoking
on the park bench. SPARKLE appears behind him,
in a robe.

SPARKLE   And you are the guy chopping wood in the New
Brunswick forest, and you have been working so
hard all day for your family, because you are
cutting wood to last the whole winter, and your
back is aching, and your hands are cold and you
are hungry, and you know there is a Russian ship
in the harbour, you've heard stories about the
sailors looking for prostitutes in Moncton and
there is a noise and you get your gun because
you think it might be a deer and you were hoping
to bring home a deer but it is a young man. A
young man with dark hair and luminous green
eyes and he is naked. He says something beautiful in Russian and although you don't understand it it brings tears to your eyes, and a warmth
fills your body. And suddenly the air is warm,
like spring, like a chinook and it flows from the
young man to you and he is looking at you. And
he is naked. He walks towards you, and you do
not move, you look into his green eyes like the
sea and he strokes your head. He runs his hands
over your face and you kiss his hands. And he
kneels beside you and he touches your chest
softly and he leans down and kisses you on the
lips. You become...

LEWIS   Stop.

SPARKLE   You haven't kissed like this for years and years,
your tongues encircling your teeth clashing, it's
as if you dived into the rough green sea together,
but there is no danger of drowning, he is–

LEWIS throws his cigarette down and walks
away.

—— 6 ——

MARGARET on the telephone with Frances.

MARGARET   Oh Frances, Frances…. There is a young person a big tough-looking Black girl running running across my yard and a Policeman is chasing her. Oh. He's tackling her. OH – she's fighting him oh the air is blue with four letter words. She must have done something terrible she looks a tough girl. WHERE is that man, that man who supposedly CARES for them all so much where is he NOW.

Ohhh yesss we are going to HANG him at City Hall.

You come and watch.

LEWIS drags SPARKLE into the office.

Well, I never know what to wear to the Opera I thought I'd wear the blue wool, what are you wearing?

—— 7 ——

LEWIS, SPARKLE, RAINE.

LEWIS is very quiet, very concentrated. He is busy with papers, money, forms as well as something he knows that could embarrass and perhaps ruin him.

LEWIS   And I told you Sparks I said if you fight Dave again I'm reportin ya to your parole officer, just watch, watch me do it. *(SPARKLE is terrified.)* You broke his tooth you asshole.

SPARKLE   But he was wearing my socks Lewis… my YELLOW ones–

LEWIS   –I don't give a shit what he was doin Sparks you know the rules. NO CONTACT of any KIND are ya STUPID? HUH?

ALL of you are SO GODDAMNED STUPID sometimes!

> *Beat. He watches him. Doing forms. RAINE runs in.*

RAINE   Um... Mr. Chance? I've got this fantastic idea; An Open House! Maybe this isn't a good time, but you know what I mean? For the neighbours? To show them we're not so bad. Like we could all bake, and Sparkle could play flute, and Dave is REALLY good on the guitar, Charlene likes to sing, I could like show them around in my best Branksome Hall English?

> *LEWIS completely ignores her, busy with his paperwork which is really frustrating him.*

SPARKLE   Oh my GOD. He's smoking again. I don't believe my eyes Lewis, Honey, I thought you were trying to quit. Put that OUT, immediately. IMMED-JUT-LY! *(tries to grab the smoke)*

LEWIS   Leave me alone. And shut up. *You* are on waivers.

SPARKLE   Export A! Sweet Jesus in Paradise! Next he's going to get a shag haircut and take up roofing!

RAINE   And like – move to Barrie!

SPARKLE   And hang out at Coffee Time!

RAINE   And wear cowboy boots with heels–

SPARKLE   –Spend welfare day at the Bingo with his five-hundred-pound girlfriend!

> *They giggle and giggle as LEWIS shuffles papers, but the shuffling almost takes on a life of it's own, angrier and angrier, he drops some, gets very frustrated and explodes.*

62 / Judith Thompson

LEWIS LISTEN TO ME YOU FUCKING LOSERS. GET OUTA MY HAIR I MEAN IT GET OUTA MY HAIR. CAN'T YOU SEE I'M BUSY? ARE YOU BLIND? CAN'T YOU SEE I'M all BY MYSELF ON THE FIRING LINE HERE? FACING A WHOLE FUCKING ARMY? LOOK AT ME I'M BLEEDING TO DEATH!

He pushes them out the door and slams it.

—— 8 ——

RAINE is at MARGARET's, mid conversation.

MARGARET *(at the window)* –Dave Hargroves at number 86 has leukemia, Ginny Lawlor at 214, brain cancer, Tara Ames' MS is getting worse day by day we used to swim in her indoor pool all winter, Dr. Denton dropped dead with a heart attack, Peggy is battling spinal cancer, Bill Henry with the lung cancer... all the wonderful and distinguished people we had cocktail parties with, and played tennis with, campaigned for the liberals and the conservatives and then the liberals again, and sat on boards with and walked our dogs with, these people are dying.

You see, I don't think any of us really thought it would happen. We didn't think anything would actually change; I was sure I would always be young, my mother would always be old. Thought I would always be carrying flowers and groceries, trailing children and dogs, dressing for gorgeous dinner parties on slate patios thought everyone would always want a part of me, "Can you run the book fair this year, Margaret, the Sunnybrook ball?" Phone would always ring mail box would always be full, eyes would always be sharp. I would always have someone telling me I was beautiful, desirable, we didn't prepare.... We didn't... expect it to happen to us, Raine, we are all, I think, deeply... surprised to find our-selves... getting old, and frail... disappearing.

RAINE   Where do you think we should go? *(pause)* No.
                 Where do you think we should go?

MARGARET   I feel very very badly about this, Raine.

RAINE   You should feel bad. You should feel very bad,
                 because you are... my GOD you are.... You are
                 doing exactly exactly what people did to Jews
                 and people of colour in the thirties and forties
                 and fifties, in this city – I did this civics project,
                 they'd say like, "Oh we have nothing against you,
                 it's just our property values" and and letters to
                 the paper saying that Jews shouldn't be allowed
                 on the beach because they leave orange peel in
                 the sand, my dermatologist, she wasn't allowed
                 into U of T med school because they had their
                 quota of Jews and the the Granite Club did not
                 allow Black people or Jewish people or Chinese
                 or anyone until like 2 years ago.

                 How is this different?

                 *Margaret looks straight at her but does not have
                 an answer.*

                 How is this different?

MARGARET   You aren't – trying – to understand – my position.

RAINE   You know what the right thing to do is, here,
                 don't you? Don't you?

                 MARGARET can't respond.

                 Well?

MARGARET   If I do... what you think is right, all my friends
                 will desert me.

RAINE   But I don't understand. If you know it is right...

MARGARET   I would be... alone. I'm 74 years old, Raine.

RAINE	But isn't it better to know that you have done the–
MARGARET	I need my friends.
RAINE	But they aren't fit to be your friends I mean, Don't you have any – criteria…?
MARGARET	These are very fine people, Raine..
RAINE	Fine? FINE? How how far would it go, if they supported Nazis, would you still be afraid to speak up? If they wore white sheets and burned black churches would you…
MARGARET	Stop.
RAINE	No. No. I mean there is a point at which all of us must take a stand, no matter what the cost. GOD is watching you right now, Margaret, and whatever you decide, that is how you will be judged.

JANET appears.

You are trying to make me homeless!

JANET	Hello there Raine. How are you doing? Are you O.K.?
RAINE	You never have to see us taking our posters off the walls, and packing our pathetic little bags, you never have to see us stand at the door of another foster home, you never see inside us to to the disruption, like like an ice storm inside the lifelong feeling that nobody wants us that we were mistakes!

RAINE looks around, desperately, and is very hurt that MARGARET doesn't rescue her.

I'm sorry, I'm sorry, I thought, I thought you were my friend, I thought that you were a decent, thinking person, the one person on this street I could trust… I thought I saw something in your eyes, something that the two of us…

(to JANET) And as to you? SHAME!

> *RAINE disappears. MARGARET crumples,*
> *JANET comforts her mother.*

MARGARET I'm just thinking of Ian. How he was always one for the underdog, A "Just Society" that's what we have always been about, starting with that marvellous Lester Pearson, your father loved him, and the Maple Leaf, and – and the notion of Canadians as peacekeepers around the world, of Canada as a model for human rights everywhere, and diversity. We were small "l" liberals, your father and I. We had dinner with Pierre Trudeau once. Did I tell you that? When your Father received the Order of Canada for his work on military history… and I do hate to see that child in pain – I'm confused, Janet. I wouldn't want your father to be disappointed in me!

JANET Mother, Mummy, you are the one who started this avalanche. And once something like this has started, it cannot be stopped. You know that, right? It's just too late to change our minds now. It cannot be stopped.

—— 9 ——

> *RAINE is in a pure rage and despair. She is*
> *cutting herself and shrieking with each cut.*

SPARKLE Ahhh. AHH!! Stop it! You stop it, NOW you stupid BITCH.

RAINE I don't care! Do you understand? I DON'T CARE about ANYTHING. Nobody wants me so I might as well just bleed to death on the floor. I hate, do you understand? I hate hate hate hate hate EVERYONE I HATE: my father, I hate my mother I hate my grandmother and my grandfather and my nonna and my poppa and my grade one teacher Miss Opal and my ballet teacher and my swimming teachers and my camp counsellors and

my riding teacher and my French immersion
teachers and my best friend Julia and my other
friend Laura every picture I ever drew those
stupid pictures she framed every dress I wore to
school every pair of party shoes every kiss and
every band-aid every Halloween costume every
Christmas present every skating lesson I ever had
every good talk with my mother I HATE my first
bra my first period and I HATE my first kiss and
I HATE I hate Oliver Moore I HATE Oliver Moore
who stole my BODY I hate Oliver Moore and
I want him to DIE I HATE my doctor and my
dentist and my friends who were never EVER my
friends and every single person at my mother's
funeral and and My MOTHER my MOTHER for
DYING and Mr. Chance Mr. LEWIS CHANCE
and you! You who don't care about anything at
all in the world except yourself and most of all
I hate myself. I hate hate hate hate hate hate
hate hate hate hate...

> *RAINE spins and spins until she collapses on the
> floor, exhausted, out of breath, sobbing. SPARKLE
> is nearby. He puts on his headphones and leaves
> the room.*

—— **10** ——

SPARKLE monologue.

SPARKLE   I care about whether I'm warm enough, or cool
enough, or good-looking enough, or if my nails
are looking raggy, or if Lewis touched me on the
shoulder, or seemed to be looking at me, or if I
want to get stoned, or my ass is itchy or I want to
eat or if Lewis thinks I'm funny but I don't CARE
about anything. Like when I see those black and
white films on educational TV about the Nazis
emptying truckloads of bodies into ditches, or
Hutu's and the Tutsi's in Rwanda and those people, those ordinary people who like turned on
their neighbours, and their best friends, and their
sisters and brothers and even their mothers

Hacking off their hands and feet, shooting old
women who are on their knees begging begging
for the lives of their grandchildren I look at their
faces and I see my own face.

He lights a sparkler and watches it burn out.

—— 11 ——

LEWIS is embracing RAINE, comforting.

RAINE   I want to die.

LEWIS   No.

RAINE   But I do, I mean what is the point.

LEWIS   No. No. That's what they expect from you, right?
Suicidal group-home girl. Are you gonna give
them what they expect? Just as they expect me to
be some high-heeled booted, gold chains, chain
smokin' nicotine-fingered eyes on the women's
chests, blowin' my nose on my disco shirt DEFY
expectation, Raine. DEFY it move OUT of your
HATE and into pure RAGE because RAGE will
ROCKET you okay? It will ROCKET you into
ACTION and ACTION is what survival is all
about. It demands EVERYTHING God GAVE you
every FIBRE of CUNNING and STRENGTH and
you know what else? *(She waits.)* The fire. That
whatsername had.

RAINE   Who?

LEWIS   You know… whatserfface… Joan, Joan of Arc!

RAINE   Who?

LEWIS   Joan of Arc, the 15-year-old French milk maid
who brought the English troops to their KNEES,
girl, JESUS you kids don't know ANYTHING
Joan of Arc? Heard the voice of GOD sayin
"*Bonjour* Joan, *ALLEZ* lead your people to a

bloody victory, *MAINTENANT la guerre* yes SIR."
Against impossible odds? Like 5000 to 1 the girl
was on FIRE. And she WON! She wasn't gonna
like collapse if somebody said she was havin a
bad hair day, right? She wasn't gonna cry if she
wasn't invited to a party, or or or if she didn't
have the Tommy jeans or a model's figure
because she had the FIRE. Her SOUL was on
FIRE. Rainers are ya with me? Are you with me?

—— 12 ——

MARGARET and SPARKLE.

*There is a loud crash. SPARKLE destroys things
in MARGARET's house.*

SPARKLE   Well... hello... Dolly, well hello... dolly it's so
nice to have you back where you belong....
You're looking swell dolly... I can tell dolly...

SPARKLE laughs until he falls down.

MARGARET   What do you want from me?

Who are you? Are you from the group home?

SPARKLE   YOU! HAVE BROKEN MY BEST FRIEND'S
HEART.

MARGARET   What?

SPARKLE   I LOVE my friend do you understand?

MARGARET   Are you speaking about Raine? That I have
somehow–

SPARKLE   You bitch! You old saggy ugly mean rich fucking
bitch!! Do you know how we hate you? We the
writhing seething K-mart masses, who mow your
lawns and clean your floors and do your hair and
your nails and sew your hems we DETEST you.
Oh my God my GOD you have NO IDEA what

you have done. YOU HAVE BROKEN MY BEST
FRIEND'S HEART!!!!

*SPARKLE falls to the ground before
MARGARET, crying, hugging her ankles –
MARGARET is stricken with true guilt.*

—— **13** ——

*RAINE has spoken for a while, this is the end of
her speech.*

RAINE And finally, Ladies and Gentlemen of city council,
friends, neighbours, if you throw us out, if you
send us away from this clean and quiet place,
with green grass and old sugar maples and well-
tended flower beds you know who you are? You
are what we have always been afraid of: you are
the bad guys, the robbers, the men in the dark the
molesters who would hang around the school,
or ask us to go for a ride and then steal our
childhood you are... the monsters in the closet
and under our beds, the pirates who drowned us
the witches who ate children! You safe and nice-
looking middle-class people who were my teachers, my principals, my doctors, and my parents'
lawyers, You! ARE what was hiding in the dark!

JANET No! No! Please, Please – We are not monsters
who eat children, we are good and caring people;
who deserve to live in peace and safety; we need
the quiet just like you do Raine. That is why we
created this neighbourhood. And you know that
there has been no quiet since the house opened,
our property values have gone down 200,000
dollars there are police sirens every day bottles
and break-ins, drugs and sex on our front lawns
we have to keep our children locked in their
homes we now KNOW that many of the teens
have been in the juvenile justice system and we
also know, most importantly that they are being
robbed and exploited by a man who we have
discovered, to our shock and dismay, has a

dizzying criminal history. *(She points at LEWIS.)*
YES.

RAINE   NO!

JANET   Yes. Yes Ladies and Gentlemen.

RAINE   NO! THIS IS NOT JUST!

                JANET and RAINE overlap.

JANET   THIS man should clearly, CLEARLY NEVER have
                been trusted with our tax dollars–

RAINE   YOU are exaggerating TERRIBLY about the sirens
                and everything and you KNOW it and and none
                of us has a perfect past–

JANET   –THIS man is nothing but a career criminal.

RAINE   –I mean I mean NOT ONE of you…

JANET   Are you ready for this?

                MARGARET runs in excited.

MARGARET   Everybody? Everybody? I have been thinking
                and… I would like to say to everyone here that,
                well, I think that the group home is… what I'm
                saying is I really do think we should all try to –
                perhaps instead of… I mean… we could we could
                give them little… I mean don't you think… don't
                you…?

JANET   Thank you, Mother, for your thoughts. Now.
                I have here, from the year 1971–

LEWIS   Sixteen years old I smuggled in smokes from the
                US of A and I made a few dollars let me tell you
                these transgressions you're gonna hear about,
                they're as long as my arm and they were many
                many years ago in a different life, I was still reel-
                ing, yes, from tragedy after tragedy within my
                family, and yah, I acted out. But THAT is why

I am qualified to help these kids, because I have
been there, Ladies and Gentlemen. I screwed up,
just as every single one of you has. Oh you may
not have been in trouble with the law, but I can
guarantee, every single one of you has broken
God's laws, your own moral laws. These are
YOUR children. You cannot abandon them. And,
most of all, you cannot send away the only person who has cared for them, the only person who
has fully, always respected their dignity, known
and celebrated their promise, and potential and
thought each and every one of them PERFECT in
their way you CANNOT exile Lewis Chance; Yes,
YES, Lewis Chance is human, does not have an
unblemished past, and hell, does not have an
unblemished present. Do any of you? In fact, I'm
still screwing up. Yah. I'll admit it.

JANET   If you don't mind, Mr. Chance, these people have
to get on with their day, and whether you like it
or not I am going to share—

LEWIS   Hell, I'll admit everything. Sometimes, you know
what? If there's some money left after the kids
have everything they need and the new wiring
and the copper plumbing is paid for and the roof
and their teeth yes, sometimes I borrow some of
that money, throw it into one of businesses, or
loan it to my mother, or one of my sisters, if she
doesn't have enough to feed her kids till her next
welfare cheque and I shouldn't do that, even
though I always pay it back eventually, I guess
I shouldn't; but who among you has not done
that with your taxes or business profits or whatever, eh? Eh? And yes I don't want any surprises
here today, I had in a way... an... unconsummat-
ed – a silent – love affair with one of my wards...
with Sparkle here; sounds like a crazy thing to
say, but I want to be totally perfectly honest here,
I have felt – desire for this young man, I have
looked at him I have even fantasized about him,
alone in my bed; dirty thoughts; he is eighteen,
true, but anyway, it's still wrong, wrong wrong
wrong, it's monstrous – to even think the thought

and I am not going to stand here tellin you to be saints, to do what is right what is true what is just when I am corroding at the edges myself. Oh yeah, I'm gay, does that scare ya? So, yeah, I crossed a couple of lines I shouldn't have, and I regret it. I will regret it till the day I die.But I'll tell ya, they will not be crossed ever again; I would do anything for these kids, you know that? I would honestly give my life. So. What are you going to do about it, are you going to throw me out?

He looks at MARGARET, walks to her, kneels down.

You. Here. You are Mapleview Lanes, you created it, you represent it, you are a fine and thinking person with a conscience, I think and I am in your hands. If you tell me to go, I will go. And if you want me to stay, I'll stay.

JANET   Mr. Chance this is inappropriate, my mother is not a well–

MARGARET   Shut-up Janet.

LEWIS   Yes?

It could go either way. MARGARET looks at her friends and she just cannot bring herself to go against them.

MARGARET   Well, it's just that I... you see I thought that instead of... but... John, Laurel, Frances... I do understand why you all feel so strongly about this and and you are my dear friends you were all so wonderful when Ian died but but after a lot of careful thought I have.... You see I think these young people are.... Oh God. I can't I can't – I just–

She walks away, full of shame, RAINE is absolutely stunned. LEWIS approaches her but

Luke Kirby as SPARKLE,
Stephen Ouimette as LEWIS,
Corinne Conley as MARGARET,
Holly Lewis as RAINE.

photo by David Hawe.

she is just as angry at him, she shakes him off and runs.

Blackout.

—— **14** ——

MARGARET and JANET.

JANET   Mum. Please look at me. I need you to look at me.
                  I need you to say thank you. All the others on the
                  block have said thank you for making their
                  neighbourhood safe again. I'm a hero to them.
                  They gave me a party. Why... why are you the
                  only one who has not said thank you?

MARGARET   Do you not feel it? Tell me, Janet. Do you not feel
                  it?

                  MARGARET leaves the room.

                  JANET is alone with her conscience.

JANET   When the kids were born it was like, the feeling
                  was oh my GOD like this... waterfall from the
                  sky. It just poured and poured over me, soaking
                  me through and and then inside me, it became
                  like this light, hundreds of thousands of years of
                  of accumulated ancient power shone out of me
                  and into my children, I felt as though I had just
                  been born, I understood God, paradise, life, all of
                  it, and it kept pouring out for 9 years. 9 years of
                  torrential powerful love I have never felt so alive
                  so present so here so mighty a queen and a
                  princess and a star and a person and then... just a
                  little while ago, when they reached about nine or
                  ten, they seemed to – to – close to me, stop stop –
                  seeing – me. Like my mother. They look through
                  me now, like she does. They flinch when I hug
                  them, they close their doors, and look away, and
                  their voices steely with the same contempt as my
                  mother – And bang, It was as if the love – the sky
                  shut like a big steel door – the flow just...

stopped. I had to work at it, I had to remind myself of how sweet they were when they were babies, I had to ignore their shallow and selfish and grasping and and whiny and cruel ways. I had to try to like them as people. As People. And it's been really... hard work. When I hear other mothers talk about how wildly in love they are with their kids I just... don't... I mean I say "yah yah, aren't they WONDERFUL" but it's a lie. There is nothing there, it's like I'm having to pump the water up from deep deep in the ground now, and I pump and I pump and it's just DRY, I look at them and I just... don't... feel – it's like what am I supposed to be feeling here? Is there something I'm supposed to be feeling? It's as if I am looking... at kitchen chairs; Okay, I know, I know, it seems as though I am saying, "I do not like my children" – But I didn't say that, exactly, did I? Because that is not something a mother can ever say. It would be preposterous, evil, no matter how many problems a mother is having with the child, she must say, "But of course I love them more than life itself." I have never heard a mother say, "I just do not like my children." And I would not say that either, I would not be the only mother in the whole world who really doesn't feel what she should be feeling for her children. I am waiting for it to happen for... the sky to open and the waterfall to pour AGAIN I am waiting, yes, until it flows down so fast and hard that I am soaked and and ravaged, with the love for my children, the waterfall drowning me *(clean, open and deep breath)*

—— **15** ——

MARGARET and RAINE in empty house. RAINE has her suitcase packed.

MARGARET has brought cookies. She stands, holding the plate out, RAINE does not take it.

MARGARET Well I'm afraid they may be a little burned on the outside it's just I had a call from my son in Philadelphia his wife is going in for surgery… they're pulling out her entire uterus…. I remembered that you said you liked peanut butter cookies, made without flour, that your mother used to make them for you… I've always found packing terribly stressful myself, somehow it gets more stressful with every year that passes… these floors are very well preserved I suppose it's the wall to wall carpeting…

I know. I know you are very disappointed in me. But I just want to say one thing to you, Raine, I want to tell you that I am truly sorry if I offended you but I made… the only choice it was possible to make because; because when I think of my will, when I think of my will in my mind I see my will is – is – a Chinese foot, I mean the foot of a Chinese woman, a geisha girl about two hundred years ago, have you ever seen pictures? They were bound, as you know, from a very early age, and and stuffed into these tiny shoes, shoes no bigger than what a four-year-old would wear. And the men, the men found these mangled stunted feet to be an aphrodisiac, and I can't explain it exactly but when I think of my own – will – I think of this gruesome, somehow sexual, mangled and malformed foot. But your own will, my dear, your own will… is… well it is…

Please don't… throw them out. I am sure they are quite… delicious… on the inside…

—— **16** ——

LEWIS, RAINE.

The house is empty. RAINE has her suitcase.

LEWIS You can hate me if you want. I screwed up. I took a gamble and I lost; we lost. And now I'm goin' back home, where I am very much needed for the

next while, and you are into a new group home
or with your Dad. Both of which will be shitty.
So. Say ya hate me.

RAINE   I hate you.

LEWIS   Good. Because I believe a young person's
intuition is pretty much perfect, like a fruit is
perfect, ya know? Ya slice open that apple and
it's perfecto. You would never question an apple.
So don't – question your apple, eh? Eh? Just keep
hating me hon because your hate is gonna–

RAINE   What? What do you think I should do with my
hate?

LEWIS   Keep fightin the fight, the fight I been fightin for
twenty years, Rainers, we need someone like you.

            *SPARKLE appears at door, with his suitcase,
            listens.*

RAINE   You are giving up.

LEWIS   No. Listen, just layin low for a bit… got things to
take care of back home, Raine,

RAINE   –HAH! You are so full of shit.

LEWIS   I'm passin the torch to you, Raine. Are you gonna
take it?

            *RAINE is disgusted. She spits and leaves. A
            moment between LEWIS and SPARKLE.
            SPARKLE approaches – LEWIS has a wavering
            moment, turns away from him. SPARKLE leaves,
            angry.*

—— 17 ——

*Sometime later, in the middle of the night. A
clandestine meeting involving RAINE and
SPARKLE; They move slowly towards each other,*

embrace like soulmates and then pick up gasoline
cans and pour in an erratic fashion around the
house, which has a FOR SALE sign on it.

SPARKLE You sure about this?

    RAINE nods.

    You know that there is… a possibility…

RAINE It's empty, I checked. It's totally empty, not even
    a mouse.

SPARKLE Five to ten years in the big House of Pain, girl!

RAINE We can't… just… be silent.

SPARKLE Hey! Hey Hey HEY. Isn't it your birthday today?

    Raine shrugs.

    Well this is your birthday candle then. Your great
    big three-story birthday candle. *"Bonne Fete a toi.*
    Bonne Fete a toi. Bonne Fete, Bonne Fete Bonne
    Fete a Toi."

    RAINE reaches, and SPARKLE gives RAINE the
    ceremonial match. They slowly walk away, and
    then turn around. They look at each other, and
    then, with a nod, RAINE tosses a match onto the
    gasoline and they watch as the house goes up in
    flames.

—— 18 ——

Lewis, in transit with a suitcase.

LEWIS At times like this it's weird. Not only can I see
    you, your tired face under my coat in the snow-
    storm? But I can hear you, trying to breathe, eh,
    it's like it's inside my ears your breathing, raspy,
    and laboured, right? Your breathing and ohh –
    your will to live.

—— **19** ——

RAINE. A few months later. In the middle of the night, is thinking back to the hospital room at the beginning; so she actually goes to the same space and light she stood in the first scene of the play. (It is best this space is purely and solely designated for only the first and last scene of this story.) Because she is remembering being in the hospital room with her mother, it is an option for her mother to actually be there. There must be a sense that time has passed since the fire.

RAINE   Remember in that story you used to read me all the time, the one I made you read me like every night when I was four? The story of the "Runaway Bunny?" The mother bunny she like would not let her little bunny run away he would say like "I'm going to turn into a bird and fly away from you" and she's like "I'm going to turn into the tree you will rest in" he's like "Okay, then, I'm going to turn into a mountain climber, and climb high high where you can't get me" and she's like "I'm going to be the mountain you are climbing on" and its like yeah. You just can NOT get away from your mother I tried. You know I did and the stupid thing is it took me this long to realize that you turned into the... air... that I breathe... I keep imagining what you would say to all THIS I would lie in bed in the jail when it was all happening and think okay what would mum have said and the thing is I – I – lay there wanting, needing to hear you to hear, actually, your voice, which is like no other voice I will ever hear, say that you know I didn't mean to hurt anybody I DIDN'T HURT anybody and it was better, I hope it was better than burning ourselves alive; and then, and then I want you to keep talking with that voice not like a knife but like like the silver of the knife a deep and dense kind of silvery – And here's what I think you are saying, wherever you are I think you are saying: If people are water and they are poured into little pots with tight lids and put on red hot elements and the heat is turned higher and higher and higher and higher they will boil over and burn your hand.

I remember now what that feels like. Not being able to breathe? To get enough air? I remember so I can feel now, what you were feeling, mother, because I went through that. When I was a baby When I was a newborn baby, 9, 10 weeks old I caught a cold, and then, after a while, the air was not reaching my body; I was trying, trying to pull it in, but something was stopping it, right? From filling my body; I became weak, like you, I was near my last breath, like you I remember... oh my mother, you are, I am...

Home.

The end.

Judith Thompson was born in 1954 in Montreal. She graduated from Queen's University in 1976 and graduated from the acting programme of The National Theatre School in 1979. Although she worked briefly as a professional actor, she became more interested in writing. At the age of 25, a workshop of her first script, *The Crackwalker*, was produced by Theatre Passe Muraille. Her work has enjoyed great success internationally. She is professor of Drama at the University of Guelph and currently lives with her husband and five children in the west Annex area of Toronto.